GOOD ★ SPORTS

*BY GLENN STOUT*

# SOLDIER ATHLETES

# GOOD·SPORTS
### BY GLENN STOUT

# SOLDIER ATHLETES

## DOING THEIR DUTY

sandpiper

HOUGHTON MIFFLIN HARCOURT
BOSTON   NEW YORK   2011

www.hmhbooks.com

The text of this book is set in ITC Slimbach.

Jacket art © 2011 Cover photographs: Ted Williams photo © Associated Press Images; Rocky Bleier photo © Associated Press Images; Carlos May photo © National Baseball Hall of Fame Library/Doug McWilliams Collection; Pat Tillman photo © Associated Press Images

*Library of Congress Cataloging-in-Publication Data*
Stout, Glenn, 1958–
Soldier athletes / by Glenn Stout.
p. cm. — (Good sports)
ISBN 978-0-547-41729-5
1. Athletes—United States—Biography—Juvenile literature. 2. Soldiers—United States—Juvenile literature. 3. United States—Armed Forces—Sports—Juvenile literature. I. Title.
GV697.A1S738 2011
796.0922—dc22
[B]
2011002095

Manufactured in the United States of America
DOC 10 9 8 7 6 5 4

4500438585

*This book is dedicated to all
my young friends and readers from
military families who are "good sports."*

# *CONTENTS*

INTRODUCTION.................................

FROM THE BATTER'S
BOX TO THE COCKPIT........................

ROCKY'S ROAD TO RECOVERY..............

CARLOS MAY COMES BACK..................

TRUE TO HIMSELF...........................

SOURCES AND FURTHER READING.........

APPENDIX..................................

.......................................... VIII

........ 1

.................................. 21

................................................ 49

............... 67

...................................................... 91

........ 95

# INTRODUCTION

**A**thletes sometimes call one another warriors, and refer to the games they play as battles, or wars.

But war and military battles are much more serious than a pickup game of football played in the backyard, a basketball game played in a gymnasium, or a baseball game played in a big stadium in front of thousands of people. War is not a game, and in the military service soldiers use real weapons. Men and women can get hurt and be killed. Peace, not just victory, is always the ultimate goal.

No one really wants to go to war or lose his or her life training for war or fighting in one. But just as athletes recognize that part of being a "good sport" is realizing that he or she has a job to do and a role to help the team win, soldiers accept a similar responsibility. Like any members of a team, they promise to do their duty for the benefit of others.

The athletes profiled in *Soldier Athletes* all sacrificed for the larger good. They gave up their playing careers—sometimes reluctantly, and at great personal cost—for a bigger cause.

*Baseball slugger Ted Williams in the cockpit, ready for take off.*

# FROM THE BATTER'S BOX TO THE COCKPIT

ON APRIL 30, 1952, some twenty-five thousand fans poured into Boston's Fenway Park. Most had come for the same reason: to see slugging outfielder Ted Williams play one final time. The previous January, Williams, who had been trained as a pilot in World War II and remained a member of the Marine reserves, was called back into military service, one of more than one thousand veteran pilots who were recalled into the service to fight in the Korean War. Williams was due to report in just a few days. This would be his last game.

Many fans thought this might be the final game of Williams's career and believed they might never have another chance to see Williams play. One of baseball's greatest hitters, Williams was already thirty-three years old and was expected to serve nearly a year and a half in the Marines. Even if he survived the war, many people thought Ted would retire from baseball after sitting out nearly two full seasons.

From the time he was a kid learning to play baseball on the playgrounds of San Diego, Ted Williams had only one dream. As he once said, "When I walk down the street, I want everyone to say, 'There's goes the greatest hitter who ever lived.'" After reaching the major leagues in 1939, Williams had gone a long way toward making that dream come true. Despite missing three seasons while he served in the military during World War II, by 1952 Williams had collected four batting titles and led the league in home runs and runs batted in four times. Ted had played in nine All-Star games, twice been named the most valuable player in the American League, and led the Red Sox to the 1946 AL Pennant and World Series. In 1941, he had hit .406 for the season. Since that time, no other player has ever hit over .400.

Most Boston fans loved Ted, and the crowd arrived early. Before the game, the club held an emotional ceremony for him on the field. Players from both the Red Sox and the Tigers stood together and held hands in a line shaped like a wing that stretched across the field from one dugout to the other. Ted was given a number of gifts, including a book signed by more than four hundred thousand fans sending

Ted their best wishes. During the ceremony, Ted stood next to Private Fred Wolfe, a veteran of the Korean War, who was confined to a wheelchair due to injuries he received during his service. At the end of the ceremony, the crowd stood and cheered as Ted turned toward the stands and waved.

Then Williams really gave them something to cheer about. With the score tied 3–3 in the seventh inning, Williams's teammate and friend Dominic DiMaggio cracked a single. The next hitter made an out, bringing up Ted.

The crowd stood and cheered again. They realized this might be the final at bat of Williams's career.

Ted looked out at pitcher Dizzy Trout and remained focused. He didn't notice the crowd and didn't stop to think that this might be his last at bat. He just concentrated on the pitcher as he wound up, and then watched the ball as it left his hand and hurtled toward the plate.

Williams saw the ball spinning in the air and immediately recognized it as a curve ball. He tracked the pitch with his eyes, and as the ball began to dip over the inside of the plate, Ted began to swing.

He hit the ball on the fat part of his bat with a slight uppercut. A loud *crack!* ricocheted through the ballpark.

As the ball left the bat in a white blur, the crowd gasped, and then kept cheering. The ball soared high and deep to right field. Tiger outfielder Vic Wertz started to chase after it but saw it was going over his head and pulled up. The ball landed eight rows deep in the stands.

Ted Williams had hit a home run! The fans cheered long and loud as the scoreboard operator showed that Williams's blast had given the Red Sox a 5–3 lead, and Williams's teammates poured from the dugout and met him at home plate.

When the game ended two innings later, Williams jogged in from left field. The next day he left for Willow Grove, Pennsylvania, to resume his military career. Ted Williams, perhaps the greatest hitter who ever lived, was now Ted Williams, marine pilot.

On December 7, 1942, the Japanese bombed Pearl Harbor in Hawaii, an event that marked the beginning of World War II for the United States. At the time, Ted Williams had just completed his third season in the major leagues. American men at the time were subject to the draft, a law that required most to serve in the military if asked. Since Ted financially supported his mother, he was not yet subjected to the draft. But by the beginning of the 1942 season it was beginning to look as if Williams, like most other healthy young men, might be drafted anyway. As he thought about serving in the military, he became intrigued with the idea of learning how to fly. So instead of waiting to get drafted, Williams enlisted in the reserves, becoming a part-time soldier. He spent the rest of the 1942 season hitting home runs by day and studying flight manuals by night. That November he reported to ground school to learn to fly.

Thus far in his short baseball career, Ted Williams had developed a bit of a reputation for being a little immature and self-centered, a player so preoccupied with hitting that he forgot about almost everything else. When he was playing the outfield, he sometimes practiced his swing instead of thinking about catching the ball. Some sportswriters criticized him for being more concerned with his batting average than with the team. They thought Williams would have a hard time adapting to the discipline of the military.

They need not have worried. Although he would have preferred to continue playing baseball rather than going to war, Ted respected military service. His father had served in the army, and his younger brother, Danny, had enlisted shortly after Pearl Harbor.

Williams was not the only professional baseball player in the military. His group of Naval Air cadets included four other major leaguers. Thousands of professional baseball players, including more than five hundred major league ballplayers, would serve in the military during World War II. Some, like Cleveland pitcher Bob Feller and Detroit Tiger first baseman Hank Greenberg, saw heavy combat, and two major league veterans, Elmer Gedeon of the Washington Senators and Harry O'Neill of the Philadelphia Athletics, were killed in combat. But most other ballplayers saw little action or were not even sent overseas. Many spent most of the war playing baseball, entertaining troops by playing on military teams. As one major league veteran later commented, "I fought the war with a bat and a ball."

Although Williams was willing to serve in any capacity, he fell in love with the notion of learning to fly an airplane, and Ted soon discovered that the same qualities that made him such a good hitter—his eyesight, hand-eye coordination, intelligence, and ability to concentrate—also made him a good soldier and pilot. He sailed through flight school, learning to fly the SNV-1, SNJ-4, and SNJ-5, propeller-driven aircraft with top speeds of between 165 and 205 miles per hour, planes primarily used to teach pilots how to fly. Ted spent hundreds of hours in the plane, learning to take off, land, and fly safely. One of his teachers later recalled Ted as "an excellent student." After earning his officer's commission, Williams applied to flight instructors' school.

He was sent to Pensacola, Florida, where he helped teach other pilots to fly, eventually becoming a second lieutenant in the U.S. Marine Corps Reserve. Although Williams was often asked to play baseball in exhibitions for the troops, he rarely appeared on the field. Teaching others how to fly airplanes kept Williams busy.

He took his job seriously. As one of his students later commented, Ted was "a very good flier." He did not act as if he were better than his students because he was a big-league baseball player. Williams knew that the students he was training were going to go on to learn how to fly combat aircraft. Their lives might depend on how effective Williams was as a teacher. Ted knew that what he was doing was far more important than playing baseball for a living.

After helping train hundreds of pilots, in 1945 Williams was ordered to the Pacific and seemed likely to see combat, but when the Japanese government surrendered on August 15, the war came to an end. In January of 1946, Williams was relieved from active duty and returned to civilian life.

He signed a new contract with the Red Sox and reported to spring training. Despite playing very little baseball over the previous three seasons, Williams showed few signs of rust and was still the same dangerous hitter he had been before the war. He led the Red Sox to a pennant and the World Series in 1946, where they lost to the St. Louis Cardinals in seven games.

In the middle of the 1947 season, Williams rejoined the Marine Corps Reserve. He thought he might like to keep flying, but he remained inactive. Once in a while the Marines used Ted to help with recruiting, putting his picture on posters, but he had no other duties.

Over the next few seasons as Williams and the Red Sox tried to get back to the World Series, Williams almost forgot that he was a member of the reserves. Williams won the Triple Crown in 1947, leading the American League in batting average, home runs, and runs batted in. He won another batting title in 1948, and in 1949 he missed winning another Triple Crown when he finished second in the race for the batting title by less than one thousandth of a percentage point. Although the Red Sox played well, they never managed to win another pennant.

Even though World War II had ended a few years before, that did not mean the world was at peace. The Korean peninsula had been ruled by Japan from 1910 to 1945. After the war, control over the peninsula was split in half, with American troops occupying the southern half and Soviet

Russian troops occupying the northern half. Although the United States and the Soviet Union had been on the same side in World War II, soon after the war ended, the relationship between the two countries cooled. The Soviet Union helped establish a Communist government in the north, and in 1950 North Korea attacked South Korea. The United States came to the aid of South Korea, and as combat intensified, the United States found itself at war again.

After World War II, the American military had scaled back. Now, as the war in Korea intensified, they had to scramble to provide soldiers and supplies for it. To make up for the shortfall, the Marines began calling reservists back to active service. They needed experienced pilots for combat.

On January 9, 1952, a letter arrived at Fenway Park addressed to Ted Williams. It ordered Williams to report for active duty in April.

Williams wasn't happy at being called back. As he told a reporter later, "I was going on thirty-four years, [and] I had already served in World War II . . . I didn't think it was fair. I didn't think it was right, to be called up again." But even though Williams disagreed, he knew it was still his duty to report. After being informed of the recall, he released a statement that said, "If Uncle Sam wants me, I'm ready. I'm no different from the next fellow." Some things were more important than being the greatest hitter who ever lived.

Two days after hitting a home run in what he thought might be his last at bat, Williams reported for active duty. As a ballplayer he had been earning $100,000 a year. Now, as a soldier, he was making only a few hundred dollars a month.

Ted first attended ground school in North Carolina and then went through cold-weather training in the mountains of California. Ted learned to fly the F-9 Panther jet fighter, a plane that was armed with 20-millimeter guns and was used primarily as a bomber.

After learning to fly propeller-driven aircraft in World War II, learning to fly a fighter jet for Ted was like going from high school baseball to the major leagues. The F-9 flew nearly six hundred miles per hour, three times faster than the trainers Williams had flown during World War II. Williams spent hours in the air and in the classroom learning the proper way to fly the plane, drop bombs on targets, fly in formation with other aircraft, and fight in combat if he was attacked.

Once again, the same qualities that made him such a good major league hitter helped him fly the jet. The jet was much more responsive than the airplanes Williams had flown previously, and he had to think and act quickly. This time, he wasn't just preparing others to fly in combat. He would fly in combat himself.

On February 4, 1953, as his former teammates were thinking about going to spring training, Williams was sent to a base known as K-3 near Pohang, in South Korea, as a member of the Marine Fighter Squadron 311.

Conditions at the base were rough, and the weather was cold and damp. Williams hated it, but he did not complain. Everybody there had more important things to worry about . . . like staying alive.

Only a few days after arriving in Korea, Williams went on his first mission, known as a fam flight—a flight designed to familiarize Williams with the surrounding area. Williams and another pilot flew their jets into enemy territory just over the front lines, and then returned to base. Although there was always the potential to be shot down or have an accident, Williams landed safely.

The next day Williams went on another mission, this time as one of five pilots ordered to bomb a rail line in enemy territory. They succeeded, dropping a total of thirty 250-pound bombs. Once again, Williams's trip was uneventful, but the danger of their task was underscored when one of the planes crashed when landing back at the base. Fortunately, the pilot was unhurt.

The following day Williams was ordered to participate in his third mission. It would prove to be the most memorable mission of his military career.

More than two hundred planes and pilots were involved. The target for the bombing run was an enemy encampment, a troop and supply area at Kyomipo. Just over twenty miles from the Pyongyang, the North Korean capital, Kyomipo was certain to be heavily defended, and all the pilots knew the mission could be dangerous.

Late that morning, Williams climbed into his cockpit and went over his usual checklist, making sure his plane was working correctly. He then patiently waited his turn before receiving the signal to take off. He turned the plane toward the runway, and when he reached position and was given the signal to go, he pulled back on the throttle. The jet came to life and rocketed down the runway. Then Williams eased the craft into the air and took aim at his target as one of a group of four planes, known as a division, that would fly the mission together.

The four planes flew toward their target, nearly an hour away, at over five hundred miles an hour. As they approached the target, Williams's division leader, as planned, went into a steep dive. The plan was for each plane to follow, dive in toward the target, and, hopefully, drop its payload of bombs and fly away before being hit by antiaircraft fire from the ground.

Williams watched the division leader's plane dive. A moment later, Ted followed him toward the target.

His plane went screaming toward the earth at hundreds of miles an hour. Then Williams pulled up over the target only a few hundred feet from the ground, dropped his payload, and started to climb. The air was already thick with smoke from bombs dropped by other pilots, and it was hard to see.

As he later described it in his autobiography, *My Turn at Bat,* Williams's plane suddenly started to shake, and "all the red [warning] lights were on." The lights told Ted something was wrong with his plane, and he soon realized it had been hit, either by small-arms fire from soldiers on the ground or by debris that had been blasted into the air by the bombs. The hydraulic system that helped him control the plane had been damaged. All of a sudden his airplane was almost impossible to control. As Williams recalled, "I was in serious trouble."

Facing a fastball with the game on the line was nerve-racking, but that was hardly a life-or-death situation. This was. In order to survive, Ted Williams would have to put all his training and experience to use.

His landing gear had deployed when he was hit, and as he tried to climb into the air, the gear slowed his plane and made it unstable. Fortunately, he managed to get the landing gear back up and started climbing away from danger. He tried to contact the other planes in the division by radio, but the radio was out, too.

As Williams climbed, he noticed that his air-speed indicator also did not work. He had no idea how fast he was flying or even if he would be able to return to an American base. He thought about bailing out and parachuting to the ground, but he was afraid he might be hurt when he ejected from the airplane. Besides, he was flying over enemy territory. If he bailed out and made it safely to the ground, he still risked being killed or taken prisoner.

Williams was actually in even more trouble than he thought. His could not see it, but his plane was leaking fuel and was on fire. A trail of smoke followed him through the sky.

Another pilot, Larry Hawkins, saw that Williams was in trouble and chased after him. He pulled his plane alongside Williams and, realizing that Ted's radio was not working, gestured for Williams to follow him. Hawkins knew Williams was in danger and decided to lead him to the nearest American airfield—if Williams's plane did not crash or run out of fuel first. Hawkins radioed the airfield to tell them he was escorting a damaged plane back to the base.

Hawkins and Williams turned back toward the American lines, climbing high so that the lack of oxygen would starve the fire.

It seemed to take forever as Williams tried to stay on course and keep Hawkins in sight, but the airfield finally came into sight. Williams began to descend and turn toward it when he heard a loud boom and the plane began to shake even more violently. As he had descended, leaking fuel had pooled up in the bottom of the plane and exploded, blowing off a wheel door. Now thick smoke was pouring from the back of the plane.

From below, the plane was a mass of fire and smoke. As the plane approached the runway, the nearby residents of a small village saw the burning plane and ran for cover, afraid it would crash into them.

After the explosion, Williams realized that he would be unable to put both wheels down, but he knew he still had to try to land the plane. He stayed calm and decided to go in for a "wheels up" emergency landing, meaning he would try to land the plane on its belly. That was dangerous in any circumstance, but because Williams couldn't control his speed, it was even more dangerous than usual. His plane careened toward the runway at more than two hundred miles per hour, twice as fast as the recommended landing speed.

As he approached the runway, fire trucks and emergency vehicles got into position below, anticipating a crash landing. If the plane caught fire, as soon as it stopped they would race in and try to save Williams, just as they would any pilot in trouble.

Williams tried to remain focused and keep the plane level as he dropped from the sky. If he came down crooked or at a steep angle, the plane would roll instead of skidding along the ground, and Williams could be killed or injured. The out-of-control aircraft might barrel into the emergency vehicles or crash into other planes and hurt or kill someone else.

Fortunately, he was able to keep the airplane straight and came in at a low angle. Still, nothing prepared Williams for the landing.

The plane hit the ground with a jolt, bouncing Williams around violently. The screech of metal hitting concrete was deafening, and the entire plane shook and shuddered as if it were falling apart. He had reached the ground, but he still had to stop the plane and hope it didn't explode.

Sparks and smoke and flames shot from the back of the plane. The only brakes Williams could use were the "speed brakes" on the wings, metal flaps that caught the air and created drag, slowing the plane. The speed brakes could not stop the plane on their own, but Williams hoped that they, combined with the friction of the belly of the plane on the runway, would stop the plane before it ran off the runway.

The plane screamed down the runway for nearly a mile, shedding debris as Williams struggled to retain control. Then, as the end of the runway approached and the plane finally began to slow, Williams realized he had one more challenge. Once the plane came to a stop, it might explode. Williams knew he would have to leave the cockpit as quickly as possible.

He opened the canopy even before the plane stopped skidding. When the plane finally jolted to a halt, Williams, never known as a fast base runner on the baseball field, dove out of the cockpit. As he recalled later, he "kind of somersaulted," then vaulted off the wing onto the ground and ran away as the crash crew raced toward the plane in trucks, ready to douse the flames.

Just as Williams had thought, moments after the plane came to a stop, it was fully engulfed in flames. Fortunately for him, by that time he was many, many yards away. The plane was destroyed, he was unhurt, and no one else was injured.

Williams knew he had narrowly avoided serious injury, or even death, and later told the press, "I was never more lucky."

Williams remained lucky. The very next day he went on another mission without incident, and over the next five months he performed another thirty-five missions successfully. Some were more dangerous than others, and on April 28, 1953, his plane was hit by antiaircraft fire, but he managed to make it safely back to the ground. In June, chronic ear trouble led the Marines to muster him out of the service.

All Ted wanted to do was hit a baseball again. Fears that he would never play again proved to be unfounded. Shortly after the armistice was signed on July 27, ending the war, Williams returned to the game he loved.

It was as if he had never left. In ninety-one at bats over the remainder of the season, he hit .407, with thirteen home runs. Williams went on to play another seven seasons, ending his career by hitting a home run in what was really his final at bat on September 28, 1961, to finish with a career batting average of .344, with 521 home runs.

Since Williams's retirement, sportswriters and fans have

wondered just how many home runs he might have hit had he not lost nearly five full seasons of his baseball career to military service. Some have even speculated that if not for his two stints in the military, Ted Williams would hold the career record for home runs.

But Ted Williams rarely complained about the cost to his career. He was proud of his service record but downplayed his sacrifice, writing in his autobiography that "I was no hero. There were maybe seventy-five pilots in our two squadrons, and ninety-nine percent of them did a better job than I did." That may have been true, but as former senator and astronaut John Glenn, who served in Korea with Williams, once said, "Ted only batted .406 for the Red Sox. He batted a thousand for the Marine Corps and the United States." The man who wanted to be the greatest hitter who ever lived was also a pretty good pilot.

*Rocky Bleier didn't let a hand grenade stop him from running.*

# ROCKY'S ROAD
# TO RECOVERY

ON THE MORNING OF AUGUST 20, 1969, Rocky Bleier was what was known as a "grunt," a private in the infantry of the United States Army. Bleier, who until recently had been a running back for the Pittsburgh Steelers of the National Football League, was now one of thousands of American soldiers stationed in South Vietnam during the Vietnam War.

Just a few days earlier, Bleier's platoon of more than a dozen soldiers had been airlifted by helicopter into the Que Son Valley in northern South Vietnam. In recent weeks the North Vietnamese Army, or NVA, had suddenly become very active in the area, and a group of American soldiers had been attacked. Ten soldiers had been killed, and another twenty were wounded. Rocky's platoon was ordered to find the dead soldiers and retrieve their bodies.

Since arriving in Vietnam in May, Rocky had been very fortunate. Neither he nor the other members of his platoon had seen much combat. Rocky was responsible for a grenade launcher, a rifle-like device that shoots grenades farther than they can be thrown by hand. So far, Rocky and his platoon had been lucky. No one had been killed or seriously injured.

Rocky's platoon had made its way through the dense woods of Vietnam the previous day and located the soldiers. Now the platoon had to find a safe place for a helicopter to land and remove the bodies so they could be returned to their families in the United States. Rocky's commanding officer spied an open, level area near some rice paddies that looked as if it would make a good place to land. He sent the platoon out to make sure there were no enemy soldiers nearby.

As Rocky and the other members of his platoon began moving from the woods into a clearing toward the rice paddies, they spread out so they would be harder for the enemy to attack. Sagging under the weight of their heavy packs, Rocky and the soldiers moved slowly and carefully out from cover. Although it was only ten a.m., the air was hot and muggy and everyone was sweating. Each man scanned the horizon as he slowly walked forward, looking for the enemy.

Just as Rocky stepped from cover, another member of the platoon began shouting. He had spotted an enemy soldier and began chasing after him, shooting as he did. Rocky and the other members of the platoon followed close behind and ran down a dike between two rice paddies.

All of a sudden Rocky and the other men heard the distinctive sound of an enemy machine gun. The platoon had stumbled into an ambush! More than a hundred NVA soldiers were dug in about forty yards ahead.

Almost without thinking, the members of the platoon dove for cover. Rocky jumped from the dike into the rice paddy, took off his backpack, and grabbed his launcher and grenades. Then, with bullets flying overhead, he crawled forward until he spotted some rustling branches that gave away the location of a machine gun nest. He loaded a grenade in the launcher, but just as he rose to fire, he felt something smack hard into his left thigh.

At first Rocky thought another member of his platoon had thrown a rock at him to get his attention. Then his leg began to sting and throb. He looked down and saw two holes in his pants and a stain of blood starting to spread.

"I've been hit!" he called out. Another soldier threw him a gauze bandage he could use to help stop the flow of blood.

Rocky wasn't the only soldier hit. One of his best friends had been killed, and several others were wounded. The next few minutes were chaotic as the members of the platoon tried to counterattack. Despite his wound, Rocky fired grenade after grenade until he ran out of ammunition.

The bursts of fire from the machine gun eventually slowed and then stopped, but every time someone from Rocky's platoon tried to move forward, the gunfire started up again. The men soon realized they were almost surrounded.

Over the next hour, they slowly crawled back toward their earlier position. Then they met up with another platoon in what they hoped was a safer location. Rocky's leg throbbed with pain, but even though the wound was serious, the bullet had missed the bone. He could still walk and crawl.

As the men dug in, Rocky's commanding officer, Lieutenant Murphy, got on the radio and called for reinforcements. Then, as Rocky sat on the ground holding a bandage to his wound, the sounds of battle began again as the enemy attacked.

This time Rocky heard not the rapid *rat-a-tat-tat* of a machine gun but the deeper, louder boom of hand grenades landing near his position. One soldier called out, "Grenade!" and Rocky saw the small bomb land only two feet away. The soldiers dove for cover a moment before the grenade exploded. Rocky was stunned by the blast but, fortunately, was unhurt.

A few moments later, however, Rocky saw a grenade fly overhead, hit another soldier in the back, then bounce toward him without exploding. The grenade came to rest at Rocky's feet. He started to jump, but before he could move, the grenade exploded.

Only one year earlier, Rocky Bleier had been a rookie in the training camp of the Pittsburgh Steelers of the National Football League. Becoming a soldier was the last thing on his mind. He was a football player. For a long time, that's all Rocky had ever wanted to be.

Rocky was born Robert Patrick Bleier in Appleton, Wisconsin, the first of four children born to Bob and Ellen Bleier, who operated a bar and restaurant together. When his son was still a baby, Bob Bleier, taking a look at his son's stocky build, called him "a little rock." Everyone began calling the baby Rocky, and the name stuck.

Growing up in Appleton, Rocky loved to play all sports. By the time Rocky started attending Xavier High School, he was one of the best young athletes in town, playing baseball, basketball, and football, and running track. In his junior year, Rocky helped the basketball team win the state championship, but Xavier's football team was even better. They went undefeated in Rocky's sophomore, junior, and senior seasons and were voted the best team in the state his junior year.

Football was Rocky's favorite sport, and Rocky, who played in the backfield on both offense and defense, was a big reason the team was so successful. Although Rocky was not very large himself, standing only five foot ten and weighing 177 pounds, he was strong and fast. In his very first high school game, he scored two touchdowns and intercepted two passes. He ran for more than a thousand yards in each of his three varsity seasons and was named all-state running back each year. The opposition became accustomed to seeing Rocky sweep around the end, dodging tacklers, or lowering his shoulder and bulling his way through the line, knocking down his opponents as if they were bowling pins. During his high school career, he averaged 9.4 yards per carry, rushing for 2,985 yards and scoring an amazing fifty-five touchdowns.

In his senior year, college football coaches began contacting Rocky to see if he was interested in playing football in college. He was. In fact, he was already dreaming of a career as a professional football player, and he knew that if he played well in college, he might get a chance to fulfill his dream.

Rocky visited several schools but was particularly impressed with the University of Notre Dame, a college in South Bend, Indiana, and their coach Ara Parseghian. Nicknamed the Fighting Irish, Notre Dame's football team was one of the most successful and prestigious in the country. Dozens of Notre Dame players had gone on to careers in professional football. When Parseghian offered Rocky a scholarship to play football, he accepted.

Rocky arrived at Notre Dame in the late summer of 1964 for preseason football practice, but at first he did not like it very much. In high school he had been a big star, but every player on the Notre Dame squad had been a big high school star. According to the rules at the time, freshmen like Rocky were not allowed to play on the varsity team. All they could do was practice.

Each day Rocky showed up and scrimmaged against the varsity team. He was amazed at the size, strength, and speed of the varsity players and wondered if he would ever be able to earn a place in the starting lineup. His dream seemed far off.

But Rocky stuck it out and in off-season spent a lot of

time working out, becoming bigger and faster. In his sophomore year, he began to get some playing time when Notre Dame was far ahead, and late in the season he even started a game when the regular halfback was hurt. Then, just before the start of Rocky's junior year, the starting halfback was injured, and Rocky got a chance to join the starting lineup. In the backfield, running for almost three hundred yards and catching seventeen passes, Rocky helped Notre Dame win the national championship. After the season, his teammates elected him team captain, and Rocky hoped to finish his career at Notre Dame with a big season his senior year.

Unfortunately Notre Dame got off to a bad start in 1967. Early in the year, the team often fell behind and was forced to pass, which meant Rocky did not get to run the ball very often. Then, just as Rocky and the Fighting Irish started to play better, Rocky tore ligaments in his left knee. He managed to finish the game, but a few days later, he had surgery on the knee. His college football career was over.

Although Rocky was a good student and was on his way to earning a degree in business management, all he really wanted to do after graduation was play professional football. But he knew his knee injury might make professional teams afraid to draft him.

On draft day in January of 1968, Rocky waited by the

phone, hoping that an NFL team would call him and tell him he had been selected. But on the first day of the draft, the phone never rang.

Rocky waited by the phone the second day, too, but once again, the phone never rang. Rocky had just about given up hope and was watching the news on television when he heard the sportscaster say "Rocky Belier, the Irish running back, went to the Pittsburgh Steelers in the sixteenth round."

Rocky was relieved, happy, and a little disappointed at the same time. While he was glad he had been drafted, he was still disappointed at being drafted so late. Four hundred and sixteen other players had been selected ahead of him. And the team that had drafted him, the Steelers, was not very good. Since joining the NFL in 1933, the Steelers had never won a championship or even a divisional title. Still, Rocky would have a chance to follow his dream . . . if he could make the team.

Rocky knew he had to get his knee in shape, so as soon as the doctors gave him permission to start exercising, Rocky got to work, lifting weights to strengthen his knee and then running. At first he could barely jog, but by the time he graduated and returned to Appleton for the summer, he was able to sprint. By the time training camp was ready to start,

Rocky was in the best shape of his life. Still, he knew his chances of making the Steelers were slim.

But that didn't stop Rocky. During training camp, he gave it everything he had. Although there were a half dozen more experienced running backs in camp, Rocky could also catch the ball, and he enjoyed playing on special teams, either returning kicks or leading the charge when Pittsburgh kicked off. He made the most of his opportunities in preseason games, and in the final days of training camp, Rocky knew he had a chance to make the team.

One day before practice, Rocky was in the locker room when one of the assistant coaches walked up to him and said gruffly, "Coach Austin wants to see you in his office."

All of a sudden there was a big lump in Rocky's throat. He knew that when head coach Bill Austin asked a player to come to his office during training camp, it usually meant he was going to tell the player he was cut from the team.

Rocky was expecting the worst when he entered Coach Austin's office. Instead he received some totally unexpected news. "Rocky," said the coach, "we got a notice from your draft board."

Service in the military has been voluntary since 1972. Before then, however, young men became eligible to be drafted into military service at age eighteen. Yet because he had been a college student, Rocky had received what was called a deferment, which meant that as long as he was attending school, he would not be drafted. But as the coach explained, now that Rocky had graduated, his deferment had expired.

Then Coach Austin told him not to worry. "We'll get this taken care of," he said. "You're good enough that you'll make the team."

Rocky could hardly believe his ears. He barely gave the military draft a second thought. He had made the team! As soon as he left Coach Austin's office, he let out a big yell in celebration.

Of course, Rocky knew the United States was fighting a war in Vietnam. It was on the news every night. Thousands of young Americans had already been killed and injured, and each day there were more casualties.

A few years before, hardly anyone in the United States had even known where Vietnam was. Then in the early 1960s, the United States government had decided to assist the government that ruled South Vietnam in the battle against the government of North Vietnam. Although at first the United States had sent only a few soldiers to Vietnam, the

North Vietnamese Army was much stronger than expected, and by 1966 nearly 400,000 American troops were stationed in Vietnam. As more and more young American men were killed and wounded, the war became controversial. By 1968 the war had heated up, and the two sides were nearly at a stalemate. It seemed as if the war would continue for years. Many Americans protested against it, particularly young people on college campuses.

But Rocky had not paid much attention to the war while attending Notre Dame. He had been focused on football. The Vietnam War had not affected him directly, and as he admitted later, "I had never thought much about military service." Even now, although he was eligible for the draft, he was not very worried about it. After all, Coach Austin had told him "We'll get this taken care of." All Rocky cared about was the fact that he had made the team.

Even though Rocky was eligible for the draft, there was still a way for him to avoid the draft and remain with the Steelers. If he joined the reserves, or National Guard, he could still play football. Although he would have to attend nine weeks of basic training and then serve periodically over the course of several years, he would not have to report until after football season was over, and then most of his duties would take place in the summer and on weekends. He might occasionally miss a game or some practice, but serving in the reserves would still leave plenty of time for him to play football. A number of other players in the NFL were already in the reserves.

Rocky began his rookie season with the Steelers as a backup running back and flanker. Although he practiced hard every week, he rarely played, except on special teams.

Still, the Steelers loved his aggressiveness and the way Rocky would sacrifice himself for the good of the team. For example, when Rocky played on the kickoff team, he would race down the middle of the field and toward the wedge of blockers running ahead of the kick returner. Instead of fighting his way through the wedge to tackle the ball carrier himself, Rocky would throw himself at the blockers and try to take down as many as possible so that his teammates, following close behind him, could tackle the runner.

He loved being a professional football player. Even though the Steelers were not very good, in Pittsburgh, Steeler fans treated the players like heroes. When Rocky and his teammates went out, they were often given free meals and drinks, and wherever they went, the players were the center of attention.

As the season went on, Rocky still believed the Steelers would take care of his draft status. But so many young men were joining the reserves that the Steelers could not find a reserve unit that had space for Rocky. He received his draft notice in October and was told to report to the United States Army on November 28, 1968.

At the last minute, some friends of Steelers owner Art Rooney offered to pull some strings to get Rocky into a reserve unit or at least keep him from being sent to Vietnam, but Rocky turned them down.

He had been doing some thinking and decided he did not want to get any kind of special treatment just because he was a professional football player. If other young men his age had to serve, so would he. Yet at the same time, Rocky did not blame anyone who found a way to keep from going to war. His brother, Dan, later became what is known as a conscientious objector, a person who refuses to fight in a war because he or she feels that killing and fighting are wrong. Even though Rocky himself wondered why the United States was fighting in Vietnam, once he decided to report for duty, Rocky had no regrets. He decided to do his duty.

In late November Rocky left Pittsburgh as a professional football player. Soon after he arrived at Fort Jackson in South Carolina, he stood in line with other recruits, raised his right hand, and said the oath of service.

I, Robert Patrick Bleier, do solemnly swear that I will support and defend the Constitution of the United States against all enemies, foreign and domestic; that I will bear true faith and allegiance to the same; and that I will obey the orders of the President of the United States and the orders of the officers appointed over me, according to regulations and the Uniform Code of Military Justice. So help me God.

The moment he said those words, Rocky Bleier went from being a young man who played in the National Football League before thousands of cheering fans to being just another private in the United States Army. After eight weeks of basic training and several weeks of specialized training in which he learned the skills needed to fight in the jungles of Vietnam, Rocky was sent to war.

When the grenade exploded, Rocky was blown up into the air and knocked unconscious. He came to a moment later and looked down at his legs. His pants were shredded, and his right leg was shaking uncontrollably. He reached down to hold it and realized his pants were soaked with blood. Pain from his right foot shot through his body. Rocky then realized that he was severely injured. The grenade had gone off almost at his feet and sent shrapnel—small pieces of metal—through his legs and right foot.

A medic cut off Rocky's boot and quickly wrapped the wound with gauze, but there was little else he could do. Like the other wounded soldiers in his platoon, Rocky needed to be in a hospital. But first his platoon had to find a way out of the ambush.

After he had been pinned down for several hours, another platoon of men finally fought their way to Rocky's position. A helicopter was waiting two miles away to evacuate the wounded soldiers.

Two soldiers carried Rocky on a stretcher until it broke. They then supported Rocky on their shoulders until Rocky nearly passed out from the pain in his injured legs. Another soldier finally lifted Rocky over his shoulder and carried him most of the remaining distance to the chopper. It was more than twelve hours since he had first been shot.

Rocky was given painkillers and then flown to a hospital where he underwent emergency surgery to remove the shrapnel. The next day or two were a blur as Rocky was kept sedated. Because the shrapnel had been covered with a chemical coating, his shrapnel wounds were incredibly painful and became infected. Then Rocky was transferred again, this time to a much bigger U.S. military hospital.

For the first time since the grenade had exploded, doctors removed the bandage from his foot to check on its condition and clean the wound.

His foot was a mess. Several toes were broken, and the foot was cut to the bone along the big toe and the instep. Infection had set in, and his foot and calf were both swollen. The doctor didn't say much specifically about Rocky's foot but told him he expected the shrapnel wounds and the bullet wound in his thigh to heal. With therapy, he told Rocky he would be able to walk "normally."

For the first time since he had been wounded, Rocky began to think about what his injuries meant for his career. If he could walk normally, did that mean he could learn to run normally as well?

Later that day another doctor came over to examine him. He knew Rocky had played football at Notre Dame. The two men exchanged a little small talk about football, and then Rocky decided it was time to ask the question he had been dwelling on for hours.

As he later related in his autobiography, Rocky told the doctor he had made the Pittsburgh Steelers. "I'd like to go back," he said. "What do you think my chances are?"

The doctor was accustomed to giving wounded soldiers bad news, and he asked Rocky, "Do you want an honest opinion?" Rocky said he did.

"Rocky," said the doctor, "you won't be able to play again."

Then, as if to make sure his patient understood, the doctor said simply, "It's impossible."

Rocky didn't know what to think. For now, he was just glad to be alive. But he didn't tell anyone what the doctor said.

Word of Rocky's injury made the news, and he received hundreds of letters from fans. Steelers owner Art Rooney even sent Rocky a telegram that read, "Rock, team not doing well. We need you."

A few weeks later, Rocky was sent to a hospital in the United States to continue his recovery. He had already made the decision to try to return to professional football. He was determined to prove the doctors wrong. He knew it would be a long road back, but first he had to get healthy.

He underwent surgery on his foot and legs several times.

Before each surgery, he told his doctors he was a football player and discussed how surgical options might impact his career. For instance, at one point a doctor wanted to amputate one of Rocky's toes. But Rocky realized if they did that, he would have trouble pushing off with that foot and keeping his balance as he ran. He convinced the doctors to save the toe.

While Rocky recovered, the Steelers helped out. They kept Rocky on the team roster, and owner Art Rooney and other members of the organization sent Rocky encouraging notes and letters. When he told them he intended to play football again, they did not discourage him. Privately, however, they thought he was dreaming. Months after being wounded, Rocky could barely walk. For him to play in the National Football League again seemed as likely as his walking across the Atlantic Ocean.

Because of his injuries, the army decided that Rocky was forty percent disabled. Instead of returning to combat, he was given light duty at Fort Riley, Kansas, where he worked in an office while he recovered.

Finally, seven months after he was first wounded, the skin on Rocky's foot healed well enough so he could begin working out. Although he knew that trying to make it back to the NFL was a long shot and that he would have to work harder than he had ever worked before, Rocky had no idea just how difficult a task it would be.

Rocky put on his workout clothes and sneakers and decided he would start to get back in shape by going for a slow jog. Even though he hadn't worked out in months, Rocky figured he would have little trouble running a mile or two.

He took a deep breath, lifted his right leg off the ground, and began to jog.

He instantly felt a sharp pain in his right foot, as if something were stabbing into his foot. At first he thought it was simply scar tissue, but with each step, the pain increased.

Rocky wasn't running—he was limping—and with each step the pain only got worse. After only a few minutes, Rocky was out of breath, wheezing, and dragging his right leg as he tried to run. Exhausted and nearly delirious from the pain, Rocky finally collapsed on the ground, sobbing. He began to wonder if the doctors were right. Maybe he would never play football again.

It would have been easy for Rocky to give up. No one would have blamed him.

But just as Rocky had felt that it was his duty to serve in the military no matter what he thought about the war, he felt he owed it to himself to give his comeback his best effort. He did not want to live the rest of this life wondering if he could play. The Steelers were scheduled to open training camp in July, and Rocky was determined to be there.

For the next three months, Rocky woke at 5:30 in the morning to run before work, then after work he spent two hours lifting weights and another hour running sprints. At first, he could barely make it around the block, and lifting even light weights left him gasping for air. But every day he got just a little faster and a little stronger.

Just before the start of camp, Rocky was discharged from the army and reported to the team.

Since Rocky had been drafted, the Steelers had changed. New coach Chuck Noll put in a new offense and defense, and with the help of some promising young players, the Steelers franchise was turning around. But Noll didn't know Rocky, and the squad included several new running backs. Bleier knew it would be a challenge to make the team.

Although he was bigger and stronger than he had ever been, Rocky knew that until the team started practicing, he would have no idea how much progress he had made.

Rocky was soon disappointed to learn that although he looked healthy, he had lost much of his speed. He was probably the slowest man on the team, and every night his foot was throbbing and swollen. He tried his best, but near the end of camp, Coach Noll asked Rocky to come to his office.

Noll was blunt. Rocky wasn't going to make the team. But that did not mean the Steelers were giving up on Rocky.

Coach Noll told Rocky to keep working out and to try again the following season. The team placed Rocky on the injured reserve list and paid him his salary so he could continue to focus on his comeback. The team even offered to pay for another operation on Rocky's foot. Although the team still did not believe that Rocky would ever play again, they wanted to give him their full support. Art Rooney promised him that even if his comeback fell short, the team would find a place for him in the front office, perhaps as a scout.

Before Rocky's next operation, the surgeon discovered that there was still shrapnel in Rocky's foot—that was what had caused the sharp pain. The doctor removed the shrapnel and also removed scar tissue that was making it hard for Rocky to run. As soon as the foot healed, Rocky started working out once again.

He went to training camp again the next season, and although he had improved a little, he was still one of the slowest players on the team, too slow for a running back. Still, the Steelers stuck with him. He was allowed to be on what was called the taxi squad. Just as in his freshman year at

Notre Dame, he spent most of the year scrimmaging against the first string. Late in the season he was allowed to play in a game, making an appearance on the punt return team, but Rocky knew he really didn't deserve to play. He was still far too slow. As Rocky himself later said in his autobiography, "If I had been the coach . . . I'd have cut myself."

In the off-season, Rocky had started selling insurance. After two long years of trying to make it back, Rocky considered giving up, but he decided to try one more time.

In the off-season he worked out even harder than before. He started doing yoga to help with his flexibility and started working out three times a day, doing sprints and even racing up and down the eight-story fire escape of his apartment building. Then he reported to camp and hoped for the best. He knew that if he failed this time, he had given it his very best.

At the start of camp, the coaching staff timed all the players in a forty-yard run. Two years before, Rocky had had a hard time completing the run in six seconds. Most running backs can sprint forty yards in less than five seconds.

When it was Rocky's turn to run, he got down in a sprinter's crouch, took a few deep breaths, and tried to relax. Then a coach blew a whistle, signaling him to start.

Rocky lifted his right leg up and out, then dug his foot

into the ground. After all his operations and hard work, he had regained flexibility in his foot, and he could feel it hit the ground and then push off.

Now his left leg reached out. Although there was still a long scar on his thigh, his leg was heavily muscled and strong. Stride by stride, his arms pumping through the air and his breath whistling between his lips, Rocky charged down the field, then crossed the forty-yard mark. He slowed to a jog and circled back to the start.

The coaches were looking at the stopwatch as if it were broken. Then one of the coaches started screaming. "If I hadn't been holding the watch," he said, "I'd ask you to run it over again."

Rocky had completed the run in 4.6 seconds. Not only was that fast enough to play running back, it was faster than Rocky had been able to run before he was injured in Vietnam!

Rocky still had to fight to make the team, but after a few good performances in exhibition season, he made the squad as a backup running back. Rookie Franco Harris won the starting job and quickly became a star, rushing for more than a thousand yards for the season. For most of the year, Rocky had appeared only on special teams, but now he knew he had earned the right to play. He was happy to contribute, but he knew he wouldn't really be back until he was in the backfield, running the ball again.

Late in the season, the Steelers led the Cleveland Browns 27–0. Near the end of the game, one of the coaches told Rocky to take the field.

For the first time since his rookie year, before he had been drafted and gone to war, Rocky was going to play running back in a regular-season game!

He joined his teammates in the huddle and listened closely as quarterback Terry Bradshaw called the play. Rocky heard the words he had been waiting to hear since that August morning in Vietnam four years before. Bradshaw called a running play. And Rocky would be carrying the ball.

The Steelers broke from the huddle, and Rocky took his place several yards behind the quarterback. Bradshaw barked out signals as the Browns' defense dug in.

The center snapped the ball, and Bradshaw dropped back as if to pass.

Rocky rose from his crouch, hesitated, and then lifted his arms up as if he were going to make a block. The play was what is referred to as a "draw" play. The quarterback drops back as if he intends to pass, and the linemen allow the defense to rush the quarterback. Then, just as the defense starts to collapse around the quarterback, he hands the ball off to a running back.

Bradshaw dropped back; Rocky acted as if he were going to block and watched as the Steelers offense line let Cleveland's linemen rush into the backfield.

Then Rocky exploded! He opened his arms and began to sprint just as Bradshaw turned and placed the ball in his belly. Rocky took it and began to run.

Before the befuddled defensive linemen could react, Rocky had already taken several steps. There was a big gap in the line, and Rocky thundered over the line of scrimmage, his legs pumping in a blur.

Cleveland's linebackers and defensive backs had seen Bradshaw drop back as if to pass and had started to cover Pittsburgh's receivers. Now they had to change direction and take aim at Rocky.

A few years before, he would have been easy to catch. But now all Rocky's hard work was about to pay off.

He ran for daylight, sidestepping some defenders, putting his shoulder down, and barreling into those he couldn't avoid. He kept his legs churning, running five yards past the line of scrimmage, then ten, then fifteen, and finally, with a tackler hanging on to his legs, through an extra effort Rocky gained two more yards. A seventeen-yard gain! Finally, Rocky was back.

*Over the next several seasons, Rocky's comeback continued. In 1975 he earned a spot in the starting lineup, and in 1976 Rocky rushed for more than a thousand yards. With Rocky's help, the Steelers made the playoffs every season from 1972 through 1979 and won three Super Bowl titles. Rocky retired at the end of the 1980 season.*

*After losing part of his thumb, Carlos May had to learn to hit all over again.*

# CARLOS MAY COMES BACK

LOOK AT YOUR HAND as it holds this book. Now look at your thumb. Just think about all the things you use your thumb for every day, from turning the pages of this book, scrolling through a website, sending a text message, or holding an ice cream cone or a pencil. You use your thumb constantly.

Now imagine that most of your thumb is gone. How would you hold an ice cream cone or a pen? Even the simplest activities would become much more difficult.

But what if you were a major league baseball player? How would you be able to hold a bat or throw a ball without the full use of your thumb?

It seems impossible. But that's just what Carlos May had to learn to do.

Carlos May was born and grew up in Birmingham, Alabama, a city with a long and storied baseball tradition. One of the most powerful teams in the Negro Leagues, the Birmingham Black Barons were based there, and the Birmingham area has sent a number of ballplayers into the major leagues, including Hall of Fame center fielder Willie Mays, who played for the Black Barons as a young man.

Both Carlos's mother and his father played a great deal of amateur baseball, and when Carlos and his older brother, Lee, were growing up, baseball was at the center of their lives. Carlos started playing when he was only four or five years old.

Lee May, five years older than Carlos, was big for his age and could hit the ball a mile. By the time he was thirteen years old, major league scouts were following his progress. At age eighteen, in 1961, he signed a contract with the Cincinnati Reds. It wasn't long before scouts noticed that Lee's younger brother, Carlos, was a pretty good player, too.

While Lee stood six foot three and weighed over two hundred pounds, Carlos was smaller and quicker. When he wasn't playing baseball, in fact, he played football, and was a star running back and punter on his high school team. In fact, Carlos was even offered a football scholarship to play for nearby Southern University.

But Carlos was an even better baseball player than he was a football player. As a high school sophomore, he hit an amazing .735, and soon the scouts were turning out in droves to watch him play. Unlike his brother, who depended on his powerful bat, Carlos was what scouts refer to as a potential "five-tool" player, a ballplayer who could run, throw, field, hit, and hit with power. Carlos could do everything on the ball field, from hitting home runs and stealing bases to making long running catches and powerful throws. In the summer he played baseball in the semipro Birmingham Industrial League. Even though Carlos was just a boy playing against grown men, he was still one of the best players in the league. Scouts from the Athletics, Yankees, and Chicago White Sox were particularly interested in Carlos.

Sam Hairston, scout for the White Sox, recommended Carlos to the team. Sam knew ballplayers. He had been a star in the Negro League, and he thought Carlos was one of the best young players in the nation. The White Sox agreed, and in 1966, after Carlos graduated from high school, the White Sox drafted him in the first round, the eighteenth player selected overall. Carlos received a $21,000 bonus to sign with the White Sox and reported to their minor league team in Sarasota, Florida.

But there was another draft on Carlos's mind—the military draft. In May of 1966 Carlos turned eighteen years old, which made him eligible to be drafted into military service. The United States was fighting a war in Vietnam, and many young men Carlos's age were being drafted into the service.

Not everyone who turned eighteen, however, was drafted. College students were exempt from the draft, and so were members of the military reserves. With his baseball career just getting started, Carlos didn't want to get drafted and then have to serve several years in the military, and perhaps even see combat, before he could start his baseball career. So, shortly after he signed with the White Sox, Carlos also enlisted in the Marine reserves.

In a sense, members of the reserves are part-time soldiers who can, if needed, be called on to serve full-time. Reservists have to go through boot camp just like every other soldier. During boot camp, young recruits learn the fundamentals of being a soldier. Living in barracks with other young men under the direction of a drill sergeant, the young soldiers undergo rigorous physical training and learn how to shoot guns and other combat techniques. Just as importantly, however, in basic training, recruits learn self-discipline and how to be mentally and emotionally strong. After all, if a soldier is sent to battle, he or she cannot just give up when things are tough. The lives of other soldiers might be at stake.

Marine boot camp is particularly tough. Near the end of training, the recruits have to go through what is known as the Crucible: a fifty-four-hour field training exercise that includes forty-eight miles of marching. After a recruit successfully completes the Crucible, he feels as if he can survive any hardship. That's how Carlos felt when he was finished.

After basic training, enlisted or drafted soldiers go on for further training. Members of the reserves, however, are released from active duty. But each month the soldiers have to report for a weekend of duty to keep up to date with their training. They also serve two weeks of annual training to ensure that they stay prepared in the event they are needed. Such a schedule allowed Carlos to fulfill his military commitment and keep playing baseball. However, like every other member of the reserves, Carlos knew that he had to report for duty when asked, no matter how inconvenient it might be, even if it meant missing some ball games. He also knew that he could be called for active duty at any time.

Carlos was not the only professional baseball player to

join the reserves during the Vietnam War. Dozens and dozens of major and minor league players were also members of the reserves. Only a few major league players, like outfielders Garry Maddox and Al Bumbry and pitchers Ed Figueroa and Jim Bibby, actually served in Vietnam.

Meanwhile, Carlos was thriving in minor league baseball. In 1966 he played for two rookie league teams, but in 1967 the White Sox assigned him to their single-A minor league team in Appleton, Wisconsin, in the Midwest League. Despite being one of the younger players in the league, Carlos was one of the best. He helped Appleton to a first-place finish and hit .338, third highest in the league, despite missing the last few weeks of the season because of his military duties. But Carlos didn't mind serving—he just wanted to play baseball.

His stellar play continued the following season, when he was promoted to Lynchburg, another single-A farm club of the Sox, but in a better league. Carlos, despite missing some occasional time owing to his military duties, continued to be impressive, leading the league with a .330 batting average. Then, at the end of the season, he heard the words every young ballplayer wants to hear. The White Sox were calling him up to the majors!

The White Sox needed all the help they could get. After

nearly winning the American League pennant in 1967, the Sox had collapsed in 1968. In particular, they had a difficult time hitting and scoring runs. They hoped a young hitter like Carlos could help.

As soon as Carlos joined the team, Sox manager Eddie Stanky put him into the starting lineup. It was time to see what the young outfielder could do.

After going hitless in his first game on September 6, 1968, in Baltimore, Carlos was in the lineup again the next day, batting third and playing left field. This time he was determined to get a hit.

He did not have to wait for long, drilling a single in his first at bat off pitcher Tom Phoebus. Although Carlos struggled after that, hitting only .179 for the season, he impressed the White Sox with his attitude. Unlike many other young men his age, Carlos took the games seriously and was disciplined. But at the same time he liked to laugh and joke and was fun to be around. He was a terrific teammate on and off the field.

In the spring of 1969, Carlos arrived at spring training hoping to make the White Sox. Even though he had been on the team the previous September, at age twenty-one, with only a few years of professional experience, Carlos knew he was a long shot. Nevertheless, he tried his best. All spring long he was one of the best hitters on the team, and when the White Sox broke camp, Carlos was named starting left fielder.

Carlos started off the season hot and then just got hotter. By mid-season he was one of the best hitters in the league and was named to the American League All-Star team to play in their annual All-Star game versus the National League. He could hardly believe he was sharing the same field with such eventual Hall of Famers as Willie Mays, Hank Aaron, Frank Robinson, Roberto Clemente, and others. The experience was made even more special by the fact that his brother, Lee, was a member of the National League team. Lee introduced his younger brother to some of the players Carlos had followed as a kid and made him feel comfortable.

Carlos made his only appearance in the game in the last inning as a pinch hitter, facing knuckle-ball pitcher Phil Niekro. The knuckle ball is a pitch that is thrown slowly, so it floats to the plate, barely spinning. Air passing over the ball causes it to dip and dart erratically. Phil Niekro, another player who was later elected to the Hall of Fame, had one of the best knuckle balls in the history of baseball.

Carlos had never even seen a knuckle ball before. He took a feeble swing at the pitch and missed it. As he later recalled, "Lee was at first base and he had his glove over his mouth, he was laughing so hard at me!" Carlos struck out, but he still enjoyed the experience. It seemed to be just a matter of time before Carlos May would make another All-Star team. If things went well and he stayed healthy, he might even make the Hall of Fame himself.

After the All-Star game, Carlos continued his hot hitting. But in August, with a batting average of .281 with eighteen home runs and sixty-two runs batted in, he had to leave the team to report for his annual two weeks of training in the Marine reserves. Although he was disappointed to leave, Carlos knew he had to do his duty. Besides, after going through boot camp, two weeks was nothing. He would be back in the White Sox outfield in no time.

Carlos reported to Camp Pendleton in California and traded his baseball uniform for dull green army fatigues. Every day he rose early and practiced the skills he had been taught during basic training.

One day at camp, Carlos was part of a group of men who were practicing firing mortars. The mortar is a long, narrow tube, about three feet long and a few inches wide, sort of like a portable cannon that stands on the ground. It takes two soldiers to operate. One, the spotter, aims the device. Another soldier, the gunner, loads it with a large explosive shell. When the mortar is fired, a firing pin hits a small explosive charge in the bottom of the shell. The exploding charge sends the mortar rocketing through the tube and into the air toward the target. The end of the mortar contains a larger charge that explodes when it hits the ground. After the mortar is fired, the gunner cleans out the barrel of the weapon.

On this day, Carlos and his partner were one of several groups of soldiers on mortar detail at the firing range. Even though it was just practice, they were still using live ammunition.

The group was instructed to fire their mortars at the same time. As Carlos later remembered, in such a situation it was sometimes "hard to tell" if all the mortars went off. After firing one round, Carlos's spotter told him to clean the mortar.

Carlos took a long iron rod with a cloth swab on the end and prepared to jam it into the end of the mortar to clean out any residue left from the blast. He had cleaned the mortar hundreds of times before without incident.

This time, however, something had gone wrong when they tried to fire the mortar. No one had noticed, but the shell had not gone off. It was still sitting in the bottom of the tube.

Carlos put the rod in the end of the tube and rammed it down so that it would reach the bottom of the gun's barrel.

*Bang!* The firing pin struck the shell. It didn't explode, but the shell still shot out of the tube. Carlos's hand was in the way, still holding on to the rod when it fired.

It shot from the cannon like a rocket. As it did, it struck Carlos's right hand.

Carlos felt a searing pain. When he looked at his hand, all he saw was red. His right thumb was a bloody stump.

A corpsman reached him within minutes and began tending to the wound. His thumb had been sheared off at the first knuckle, and the rest of the thumb, a mass of bone and raw flesh, had been struck with such force that it was bent backwards and embedded in his wrist.

The corpsman helped Carlos to a car. When he climbed inside, Carlos passed out from the pain and shock. The corpsman rushed Carlos to the hospital. Another major league player at the camp, Bob Watson, actually found the remnant of Carlos's thumb and turned it over to the doctors, but it was too damaged to be reattached.

The doctors performed emergency surgery on Carlos. When he awoke and saw his hand swathed in a huge bandage, he thought, "Well, there goes my career." At age twenty-one, he feared that he would never play baseball again.

But as he looked around the hospital ward, nearly every other bed was occupied by soldiers who had been injured in Vietnam. Carlos later recalled, "When I first went to the hospital, I felt sorry for myself. Then I looked around. I saw guys with no eyes, guys with no legs, guys with half a head, guys who couldn't talk, hear, guys with no mind or half a mind. I began to think, 'What am I griping about?'"

Carlos was just glad to be alive. He had actually been a little bit out of position when he had jammed the iron rod down the barrel of the mortar. "If I had been doing it right," he said later, "I would have been looking into the mortar and I would have had my head blown off." Considering what could have happened to him—and the more significant injuries suffered by soldiers who had been hurt in combat in Vietnam—put everything in perspective.

Over the next few days, a series of doctors looked at Carlos's thumb. Although one said to him "Maybe you better forget baseball," by then Carlos had another idea. After all, he was a Marine, and he loved baseball. He wasn't going to let anything stop him. When his wife, Margaret, arrived at the hospital, he told her, "Get me a box of balls for when I get home." He was determined to play baseball in 1969. "I love to play the game, and I intend to play the game," he told a reporter only a few days after the accident. "I just want to get out of the Marines to put my full time in baseball."

Carlos's doctors, however, were not so sure. "We'll have

to do a closure at the top of his thumb," explained one doctor. The blast had torn off the entire top of his thumb, and
they would have to graft skin from elsewhere on his body
just to close the wound. "The loss of the distal portion [first
joint] of his thumb will have some effect on his ability to
play baseball again. But it is too early to assess the effect."

After the first operation, the White Sox got involved and
had hand specialists take a look at Carlos's thumb. Over
the next few months, Carlos underwent four separate operations as doctors rebuilt his injured digit.

One surgery in particular stood out. To help grow skin to
cover Carlos's thumb, the doctors actually sewed his thumb
and hand to his stomach. Carlos spent weeks unable to move
his arm freely. He was right-handed, and even the simplest
tasks, like buttoning a shirt or tying his shoes, were difficult.
Then, after skin from his stomach grew onto his thumb, they
cut his thumb and hand loose and sewed up both wounds.

By January, Carlos was finished with surgery, and the
Marines released him from his service duties. With a bad
thumb, he wasn't much use as a soldier. Carlos hoped that
wasn't true as ballplayer.

With spring training ready to begin less than two months
later, Carlos knew he had a lot of work to do. His hand, as
one writer described it, "looked like a badly sewn mitten."

His thumb was only half as long as it had been. There was no fingernail, and the remaining portion of the thumb was still red and stiff and swollen. The new skin was still tender.

Just as Carlos had asked, when he returned home, Margaret had a box of baseballs waiting for him. Carlos wasn't too worried about being able to hit. Although he was right-handed, he hit from the left side. Enough of his thumb remained that he could still hold the bat in the space between his thumb and palm. "I might have to cut down on my stroke a little," he said, "but I know I can bat."

Throwing, however, was a different story. You throw a baseball with the thumb resting underneath the ball. Throwing without using your thumb is almost impossible.

But that didn't stop Carlos. At first he and Margaret just rolled the ball back and forth along the ground. Carlos taught himself to pick it up and soon became used to the different way the ball felt in his hand. He couldn't grip the ball as tightly as before, but he could still pick it up. "She rolled it to me by the hour," he said later. "She's got a lot of guts." Then he started playing catch. It wasn't easy, but Carlos discovered he could still throw. Each time he did, he found he could control the ball a little bit better than before.

However, being able to play catch with his wife wasn't

quite the same as playing in the major leagues. Carlos really wouldn't know if he could play until spring training.

He arrived at camp and slowly began working himself back into shape. When he went to take batting practice for the first time, on the very first pitch he swung at, he tore the skin on his thumb wide open. Fortunately, the White Sox helped out. They had a special batting glove made that helped protect his thumb, and over time the skin toughened.

He played surprisingly well in the spring, but Carlos knew that until he proved he could play in the regular season, he still wouldn't be certain of his recovery.

The White Sox opened the season in Chicago on April 7, 1970, versus the Minnesota Twins. Although the air was cold and there were only a little more than 11,000 fans in the stands, to Carlos it felt as if Chicago's Comiskey Park were full. Today he would discover if he could really play.

Batting third, Carlos came to bat in the first inning with two men on base. When the announcer called out his name, everyone in the stands stood and cheered. "That was beautiful," he said after the game, "and it made me play harder." Unfortunately, Minnesota pitcher Jim Perry struck Carlos out. Carlos would need to get a hit to prove to everyone that he was really back.

In the fourth inning, he got another chance. Now, after playing several innings in the field, he was not so nervous. He wasn't thinking about his thumb. He was simply playing baseball, just as he had since he was a young boy, playing with his brother and his parents back in Birmingham.

Carlos led off the fourth inning. Jim Perry was one of the best pitchers in the league. Carlos knew he wouldn't take it easy on him, and he didn't want him to. He tried to stay calm and focus on the ball.

A pitch came in out and over the plate. Carlos kept his eye on the ball and heard the sweet sound the bat makes when it strikes the ball.

The ball rose on a line toward the second baseman, then rocketed over his head and landed in the soft grass of right center field. Carlos dropped his bat and raced to first, taking a small turn toward second as the Minnesota outfielder retrieved the ball. Then Carlos turned back to first, stepped on the base, and stood there as the crowd roared. He was back.

Later in the game, he made several plays in the field and even had to make a long throw. There was no doubt that he could still play.

He was appreciative afterward, telling a reporter about his base hit that "Yes, I'll remember it a long time . . . This was playing for keeps, and I've been thinking a lot about that for a long time."

Carlos went on to play another seven years in the major leagues, and then four more in Japan before going to work for the postal service in Chicago. Although he never quite hit with the same power he had before his accident, and he eventually began playing some first base so he would not have to throw the ball so far, he remained a very valuable player. He finished the 1970 season with twelve home runs, sixty-eight RBIs, and a .285 batting average. The following year he finished seventh in the league in hitting and was fourth in 1972, when he was again named to the All-Star team. He played in the World Series for the New York Yankees in 1976.

Although some baseball historians have since said that Carlos's injury might have prevented him from having a Hall of Fame career, Carlos May never worried about what might have been.

Incredibly, Carlos actually came to believe that the injury was a good thing. "It actually made me a better hitter," he later said. "I choked up on the bat afterwards and used all the fields." After all, compared to what might have happened to him, "What right did I have," he said, "to squawk about losing a little bitty tip of my thumb?"

*Pat Tillman was more than just a football player.*

# TRUE TO HIMSELF

PAT TILLMAN had it all.

When Pat Tillman went to training camp with the Arizona Cardinals in the summer of 2001, he was on top of the world. Preparing to begin his fourth season of professional football, Tillman was the Cardinals' starting safety, about to marry his high school girlfriend, earning more than half a million dollars a season, and just starting to be recognized as one of the best defensive players in football. Although Tillman, only five feet eleven and 198 pounds, was small for a professional football player, fans loved his drive and energy. Fast and tough on the field, Tillman had a reputation as a hard-nosed player who always gave his best effort. One of the best tacklers in the league, Tillman went up against players much larger than he and never backed down.

But Pat Tillman was more than just a football player. Although he loved playing football, it was not his entire life. He was curious about the world, and when he wasn't playing football, Tillman was as likely to read a book as he was to work out, or go for a hike instead of going out to a nightclub. He awoke each day excited about the possibilities that life offered, and he looked forward to new challenges.

Growing up on a country road in New Almaden, California, with his father, Pat Senior, mother, Mary, and younger brothers, Kevin and Richard, as a toddler Pat was precocious. He started walking when he was only eight months old, and as soon as he learned to talk, he jabbered constantly. The Tillmans rarely allowed their children to watch television. Instead, his mother often took the boys on long walks exploring the park close to their house, a near-wilderness area crisscrossed with more than thirty miles of trails. The young boys loved scrambling over the countryside, climbing trees and seeing what was around the corner on the trail.

As his father once told a reporter, even as a young boy, Pat "always liked testing himself." When he was five years old, his mother once discovered him high in a tree next to the Tillmans' house, clinging to the trunk as the tree swayed back and forth during a windstorm. Fortunately, she was able to help him climb to safety.

The Tillmans channeled Pat's energy toward sports, and at age four he began playing organized soccer. Pat's mother served as his coach. But when Pat began seventh grade, he decided he wanted to play football instead. Despite breaking his leg in one of his first games, by the time he reached high school, he had fallen in love with football.

Although Pat was a few inches shy of six feet tall and weighed well under two hundred pounds, as a sophomore at Leland High School he made the varsity team. Despite his relatively small size, he was bubbling with energy, and his coach couldn't keep him off the field. He played almost every position but lineman. On defense, he played safety and linebacker; on offense, he played running back and wide receiver; and on special teams, he was the punter and ran back punts and kickoffs. One time, after Pat's team finished the first half with a big lead, his coach told Pat he would not play in the second half. But Pat wanted to play so badly he sneaked back onto the field and returned a kick for a touchdown. To keep him from doing it again, his coach took away his helmet and hid it under the team bench.

Pat wanted to play Division 1-A college football, the

highest level, but the odds were against him. Although he was a star in high school and had grown to stand five feet eleven and now weighed just less than two hundred pounds, few Division 1-A schools were interested. Only six percent of all high school athletes get to play sports in college at any level, and even though Pat was talented, most coaches thought he was a little slow to play in the backfield in college, too small to be a receiver, and not big enough to play linebacker. Only a handful of schools showed any interest in him.

Then Pat almost blew it. The night after the final regular-season game of his high school career, a win that put Leland into the playoffs, Pat was at a pizza restaurant with members of the team. Someone ran inside and told the group that one of Pat's friends, a young man who had a skin condition that resulted in disfiguring scars, was getting beaten up in a fight outside. His skin was easily torn and put him at a huge disadvantage in a fight.

Without thinking, Pat raced outside the restaurant to defend his friend. He saw someone running away and lost control. Pat attacked him, knocking the young man to the ground and then kicking him over and over again. The police showed up, and then Pat realized he had made a big, big mistake.

The man he had attacked had not even been involved in the fight. Once Pat saw that he had hurt the young man badly—he had given the man a concussion, knocked out several teeth, and caused his eye to swell shut—Pat realized that he had been wrong to react to violence with more violence in the first place. He felt terrible. Instead of trying to run away from the police or make an excuse, Pat admitted that he had been in the wrong and apologized to the young man.

Fortunately, the other young man was not permanently hurt, although he did have to have dental work done on his teeth. The victim pressed charges, and Pat was charged with a felony and had to go to court. In the meantime, the University of Arizona, unaware of the incident, decided to take a chance on Pat and offered him their last available scholarship. But according to the terms of the scholarship, if Pat was convicted on a felony charge, he would have to tell the university and they could take away his scholarship.

Fortunately for Pat, the judge, realizing that Pat accepted responsibility for his mistake, reduced the charge to a misdemeanor, which allowed Pat to keep his scholarship. Still, Pat's family had to pay the young man forty thousand dollars, and Pat was sentenced to thirty days in a juvenile facility plus 250 hours of community service. His did his time, worked at a homeless shelter, and was able to keep his scholarship.

His conviction was a life-changing experience. While serving his time in the detention center, Pat reassessed his life. "It made me realize that stuff you do has repercussions," he later told a reporter, adding, "You can lose everything." Pat had always been a B and C student before the incident, but while in the detention center, he began reading to pass the time and fell in love with learning. "I'm proud of that chapter in my life," he said later. "I'm not proud of what happened, but I'm proud that I learned more from that one bad decision than from all the good decisions I've ever made." Pat was never in another fight.

Pat reported to school in Tempe, Arizona, in August. He met with coach Bruce Snyder, and Snyder told him that he might be "redshirted" as a freshman, meaning that he might not play his first season but would still be eligible to play another four seasons if he stayed in college for a fifth year.

Pat looked at the coach as if he were crazy. Tillman did not plan to take it easy in college. "I've got things to do with my life," he said. "In four years, I'm gone." The coach had never seen a freshman with so much confidence.

Pat's attitude extended to his play on the field. He made the team as a freshman and made his mark on special teams, playing all out and performing as if every play were his last. In his sophomore season, despite his small size, he began to see some playing time at inside linebacker, and although he started only one game, he was sixth on the team in tackles.

Even though Pat was succeeding on the field, he was getting more out of college in the classroom. Many college football athletes are so focused on the game that they take an easy class schedule and do just enough work to get by. Some take the bare minimum number of courses needed and end their college football careers well short of the number of credits needed to graduate.

Pat, however, was more than the stereotypical "dumb jock." Pat took his classes seriously. Everyone at school knew he was a football player, but in class Pat surprised everyone by being involved. He loved talking about history and politics and a thousand other subjects, and he often stayed up late talking with his classmates. He developed the habit of always carrying a book with him and using every spare moment to read. After earning a solid 3.5 grade point average in his first semester, Pat's classroom performance steadily improved. A marketing major, Pat still took courses in other subject areas.

In his junior season at Arizona, Pat earned a place as a

linebacker in the starting lineup. The Sun Devils, after going 4–7 in Pat's freshman season, went 7–4 his sophomore year and hoped to improve in 1997.

They opened the year with two wins, and then faced powerful Nebraska. The year before, Nebraska had beat them 77–28. Pat and his teammates were determined to get revenge.

Pat led an aggressive defense that never allowed the Cornhuskers to get on track. In the first quarter, Pat helped cause a fumble and then helped bat the ball out of the end zone for a safety. Later in the game he sacked the quarterback in the end zone for another safety. The Sun Devils shut out Nebraska, winning 19–0. Exuberant Arizona fans tore down the goalposts after the game in celebration.

Arizona went undefeated in the regular season and, with a possible national championship at stake, played Ohio State in the Rose Bowl. Pat played well, but the Sun Devils fell 20–17. Still, Pat's performance over the course of the season, in which he led the team in interceptions, fumble recoveries, and pass deflections and was second in tackles, set him apart. He entered his senior year as one of the best defensive players in college football.

But football continued to be only a part of Pat's life. In the summer, instead of taking it easy, Pat took classes. He liked to go rock climbing with his friends and enjoyed diving from high bridges and cliffs into the water. Sometimes he would even go into the woods, climb a tree, and see how far he could travel climbing from tree to tree before he came back down to the ground.

Despite the fact that Arizona lost many players to graduation before Pat's senior year, he still led the Sun Devils to a respectable 9–3 record. The magazine *Sports Illustrated* did a big story on Pat, and writer Tim Layden wrote, "This season Tillman has simply become the best player in the country." Pat led the team in tackles and was named the defensive player of the year for the Pac-10 conference. Moreover, he graduated from college in only three and a half years, accumulating a stellar grade point average of 3.84. As one of the Arizona football coaches said of him, "He epitomizes what college football is all about."

Pat hoped to play professional football, so he spent the rest of the winter and spring working out to prepare himself for what are called "combines," large, organized workouts for aspiring professional football players. Representatives of each pro team show up at the combines and watch as players are timed in sprints, lift weights, and perform other physical tests of skill, speed, and strength.

Pat knew that playing in the NFL was a long shot. Only

one percent of Division 1-A college football players makes an NFL roster, and even though Pat had been a successful college player, at only five feet eleven and 195 pounds, he was far too small to play linebacker in pro football. He had the skills to play in the defensive backfield, but he was not as fast as most other NFL backs.

While Pat impressed NFL scouts with his intensity, his times and scores at the combine were not very impressive. On draft day, 225 other players were selected before the Arizona Cardinals took a chance and drafted Pat in the final round. He quickly signed a contract and received a modest bonus of $21,000 to sign, but if he got cut from the team, he would receive nothing more.

Yet from the moment he stepped onto the field at training camp, Pat played as if it were his last game. While many players were working their way into shape and playing cautiously to keep from getting hurt, Tillman played as hard as he could. During the exhibition season, he not only led the team in tackles but surprised everyone when he earned a place in the starting lineup. Although he lost his starting job toward the end of the season after making some rookie mistakes, Tillman still received a lot of playing time, and the Cardinals made the playoffs.

After spending most of the 1999 season playing on special teams and on the second string, by the end of the season he worked his way back into the starting lineup. In 2000 he secured the position and reestablished himself, setting a new team record with 224 tackles during the sixteen-game regular season. Although the Cardinals finished only 3–13, NFL insiders recognized that Tillman was becoming one of the best safeties in the league.

At the same time, however, Pat Tillman began looking for new challenges. Now that he knew he could play in the NFL, he wondered what else he could accomplish. Before the 2000 season, he trained for a marathon, running the 26.2-mile race in less than four hours, a good time for a first-time marathoner. He and his girlfriend, Marie, also went to Europe, traveling through Germany, France, Switzerland, and Italy. Pat wanted to see every museum and try every kind of new food and new experience he encountered.

After the 2000 season, Pat's contract with the Cardinals, who had paid him the league minimum for a third-year player, $361,500, expired. Tillman was a free agent and could sign with any team in the league.

Based on his performance, he got the attention of the best team in the league, the NFL champion St. Louis Rams. The Rams had a reputation as a great offensive team but one that needed to be a little tougher defensively. Their coaches thought Pat would fit in perfectly. In April they contacted Pat's agent and offered him a five-year contract for $9.6 million, including a $2.6 million bonus!

That was enough money to set Pat up for the rest of his life. Pat's agent knew the Cardinals could not afford to match the offer and told Pat he should sign with the Rams. He could not imagine anyone turning down such a spectacular offer.

But Pat wasn't like anyone else. He liked making money, but it was more important to Pat that he stay true to himself. He liked playing in Arizona with the Cardinals. He liked his coaches, liked his life there, and liked the challenge of playing for a team that was trying to become a championship team.

A few days later, Pat called up his agent and calmly turned down the deal. "I'm going to stay with the Cardinals," he said. They had believed he could play in the NFL when no other team did, and Pat appreciated that. His agent thought he was crazy, but Pat didn't care. He thought values like loyalty were more important than money.

In the off-season, Pat sought out another challenge, this time competing in a triathlon, a competition that includes three events—in this case, a 1.2-mile swim, a 56-mile bike ride, and a 13.1-mile run. Pat completed the triathlon in just over six hours. Although that was two hours behind the leaders, Pat was still pleased that he had successfully completed another personal challenge.

Training for the triathlon left him in great shape for the 2001 season, and Pat looked forward to having a big season. A few days before the Cardinals' first game, on the morning of September 11, 2001, Pat was asleep when his phone rang.

It was his brother Kevin. From the panicked sound of Kevin's voice, Pat could tell something was wrong. "Turn the TV on!" his brother yelled.

Pat turned on the television, and, like millions of people all around the world, he was transfixed and horrified by what he saw. Over and over again he saw video of two commercial airplanes that had been hijacked slamming into the twin towers of the World Trade Center in New York City. Hundreds of people on the planes and in the towers were killed by the impact, and over the next few hours, as the towers burned and then collapsed, nearly two thousand people lost their lives. A terrorist group known as al-Qaeda, which blamed the United States for political problems in the Middle East, was behind the hijackings.

Like many other Americans, Pat spent the next few days in a daze as the news covered the efforts of police, firemen, construction workers, and others to find survivors in the burning pile of rubble at Ground Zero. While the nation mourned, the NFL, like major league baseball, suspended play.

Just as the fight during his senior year of high school had caused Pat to step back and reassess his life, so did the events of September 11. He was just a football player, and as he told an interviewer at the time, "It is so unimportant compared to everything else that is taking place." The United States soon began military action in Afghanistan, where the hijackers had been trained, in response to the attacks.

Nevertheless, when the season resumed, Pat played well, even as the Cardinals struggled to a 7–9 record. But Pat continued to wonder just how valuable it was to be a professional football player. Football just did not seem very important.

He was restless in the off-season, going skiing and rock climbing and planning his wedding with Marie, but he felt that something was missing in his life. Like Pat, his brother Kevin, a minor league baseball player, also questioned the value of being a professional athlete. He knew watching football made people happy, but playing the game just didn't seem important compared to some other professions. Since the attacks, the two brothers had spent hours discussing how they could live more meaningful lives.

The answer came from their family. There was a long tradition of military service in the Tillman family. Pat's grandfather Henry Tillman had been in the navy and stationed on a destroyer in Pearl Harbor in Hawaii when the Japanese attacked, sparking the involvement of the United States in World War II. His two uncles had been stationed nearby in the army, and one was later wounded. His other grandfather, Richard Spaulding, had served as a Marine in Korea. In the months after 9/11, Pat and his brother began discussing joining the military. After the end of the football season, those conversations began to be more serious.

Late in the spring of 2002, Pat and his brother made the decision to enlist together. As Pat wrote, he had decided that even though "my life at this point is relatively easy . . . it is not enough." The more he thought about it, the more he found that life as a professional athlete was "shallow and insignificant." Besides, his conscience was now calling him "in a different direction." By joining the military, the two brothers thought they could help their country and that their lives would have more significance.

Each gave up the life of a professional athlete in favor of

the life of a soldier. Instead of wearing the uniform of their team, they would wear the uniform of their country. Instead of staying in hotels and being cheered by fans, they would sleep on cots in a barracks and get yelled at by a drill sergeant. And instead of earning the salary of a pro athlete, they would earn the salary of a soldier. For Pat, that meant a pay cut from more than half a million dollars a year to only $17,316.

After studying their options and speaking with military recruiters, Pat and Kevin decided to enlist in the army. They decided to try to become Army Rangers, members of an elite Special Operations Force. They were not interested in just becoming soldiers and then ending up sitting behind a desk somewhere. By becoming Rangers, they knew they would be tested and would likely face combat in Afghanistan.

As they had planned, Pat and Marie were married on May 4, 2002. After a honeymoon in the South Pacific, in June Pat, aged twenty-five, and Kevin, twenty-four, enlisted in the army and were ordered to report to basic training on July 8, 2002.

When word of Pat's decision reached the public, it became a big story. Almost overnight he received dozens and dozens of requests for interviews. Book publishers wanted to publish his life story, and movie producers wanted to make it into a movie. They offered Pat huge sums of money for his story.

But Pat had not joined the army to get publicity or earn thousands of dollars. In fact, the idea of doing so disgusted him. He turned down every single interview request and ignored offers from book and movie companies.

Pat and his brother went through basic training and then specialized training to become Army Rangers. It did not take very long for Pat's commanding officers and fellow soldiers to discover who he was, and it sometimes made his life tough. Some gave Pat and his brother a hard time because they were well known, but Pat never tried to act like a big shot. Just as he had to make his way into the starting lineup on the football field by his performance, Pat knew he would have to earn everyone's respect in the army by the way he performed as a soldier.

Army Ranger training is some of the toughest training that takes place in the army. The two-month course is designed to challenge the recruits in every possible way. Conditions are tough, and the candidates are taught leadership skills as well as combat skills in mountain, jungle, and desert environments. They often remain active and awake for hours at a time and are provided with only the most basic supplies. They train in all kinds of rough weather and get very little rest. Many soldiers quit before the end of training or are asked to leave. Only about half of those who begin training to become a Ranger succeed.

Pat and Kevin both made it through the first phase of Ranger training, the Ranger Indoctrination Program. They expected to be sent to Afghanistan soon.

But in March of 2003, the United States, telling the American people that Iraqi dictator Saddam Hussein possessed weapons of mass destruction like nuclear bombs and chemical weapons, invaded Iraq. That turned out not to be true, and both Pat and his brother questioned the wisdom of invading Iraq, but as soldiers each did his duty and followed orders. They were ordered overseas. At first it looked as if they might participate in the initial invasion, but at the last minute, the plans were changed. The two brothers ended up spending about two months in Iraq but saw no combat. Most of the time they were stationed in Baghdad in a supporting role.

Although Pat was happy to be returning home safe, he was disappointed by the experience and felt he had not been very useful. Upon their return, both Pat and his brother entered Ranger School, the most difficult and grueling part of Ranger training. The nine-week program entailed a series of twenty-hour days of field training near Fort Benning,

Georgia. Although nearly half of their class of 253 soldiers failed or dropped out, Pat and his brother both passed and became full-fledged Rangers, earning promotions from private to specialist.

In the meantime Pat's agent was being contacted by NFL teams who wanted Pat to play football again. Since he had already served overseas, some people in the NFL told Pat's agent they could pull some strings and arrange for him to be discharged early.

Pat would not hear of it, telling his agent, "I enlisted for three years. I owe them three years." He remained in the army, and in April of 2004, both Pat and Kevin were sent to Afghanistan.

Soon after their arrival, Pat and his platoon, known as the Black Sheep, were ordered out on their first mission. Along with several Afghan soldiers, they were sent on a "sweep and search" mission to seek out the enemy near the border with Pakistan.

For several weeks the patrol was uneventful. Pat's platoon did not encounter either members of al-Qaeda or members of the Taliban, a terrorist group that had governed Afghanistan before being ousted by American troops in 2001. Both the Taliban and al-Qaeda were regrouping and in hiding in the rough, mountainous terrain of eastern Afghanistan.

They were far more familiar with the area than U.S. troops and were difficult to find.

On April 13 Pat's platoon of thirty-four soldiers, including his brother, was on patrol. Their orders were to go to the village of Manah and search for the enemy. But on their way, one of their armored vehicles, known as a humvee, broke down. They sat in place for hours, and the platoon fell behind schedule.

Pat's commander eventually split the platoon in two. One group that included Pat, known as Serial One, went ahead toward Manah. Another group, Serial Two, remained with the vehicle. They eventually were able to hire a local Afghan with a tow truck to move the vehicle, and followed Serial One toward Manah.

Early that evening, the sun was beginning to set and the mountains cast long shadows over the ground. In the twilight Pat and the rest of the men in Serial One, following a dirt road, entered a steep, narrow canyon.

The surroundings made the men nervous. The sheer walls of the canyon reached to the sky, and it was impossible to see very far ahead or know if anyone was lying in wait for them. It was the perfect spot for an ambush.

They moved quickly but carefully through the canyon and breathed a heavy sigh of relief when they made it through without being attacked. Only a few minutes later, Serial Two, towing the humvee, entered the canyon.

None of the men knew it yet, but while the humvee had been broken down, they had been spotted by the enemy. Now, as Serial Two slowly entered the canyon, the enemy, hidden nearby, fired a mortar into the canyon.

*Boom!* The ground suddenly exploded in the canyon, and rocks blown into the air by the blast rained from the sky. The men in Serial Two dove for cover. Within seconds, two more mortars exploded. Serial Two prepared for battle.

Up ahead, Serial One heard the explosion and realized what was happening. Pat and the rest of the men began moving back toward the canyon to help out.

In the narrow canyon, it was impossible for Serial Two to make radio contact with Serial One, and in the dwindling light it was impossible to see clearly for more than a few yards. Serial Two had no idea that Serial One was coming back to help.

Keeping an eye out for the enemy, Serial One worked its way back toward the canyon, not knowing if the enemy was now waiting for them as well. Then Pat and several others reached a ridge at the edge of the canyon. Looking down into the canyon from less than one hundred yards away, they could make out the outline of the humvee and could see men moving. They waved their arms to get the attention of Serial Two and let them know they were nearby.

But down in the canyon, the men of Serial Two misinterpreted the waving arms. They thought Pat's group was the enemy and started firing at them.

The next few moments were chaotic. The men on the ridge took cover and started yelling "Cease fire, cease fire!" But the sounds of gunfire drowned out their calls. It was a dangerous situation. Serial One was now under attack by Serial Two.

Pat, however, stayed calm and thought quickly. After all, that was what he had been trained to do. And now, at just the right time, it seemed as if he had a solution.

"I've got something that can help," he said to the other men. Then Pat lit a smoke grenade, hoping that when the soldiers of Serial Two saw the familiar purple smoke of the grenade, they would realize they were firing on their own soldiers and stop.

As the smoke billowed into the air, it seemed to work. The shooting stopped, and Pat and the others began to move from cover.

Then, without warning, the shooting started again. As soon as it did, Pat and the others started yelling again. Pat started screaming, "What are you shooting at? I'm Pat Tillman! I'm Pat Tillman!"

Then his screaming stopped. The Ranger next to Pat Tillman looked down and saw that his friend was dead. Pat had been shot in the head and killed.

A few minutes later, the shooting stopped. Serial Two left the canyon and eventually linked up with Serial One. It was only then that they realized they had been shooting at their own men. Another soldier told Kevin Tillman that his brother was dead.

Pat Tillman's death became a big news story. Unfortunately, instead of admitting that Tillman had been killed in a "friendly fire" accident, because Pat was famous, the U.S. Army lied about the circumstances of his death, saying that he had been killed by the terrorists as he directed an attack.

Pat's family knew better. After all, Kevin had been nearby. They were crushed by Pat's death, but being lied to made it even worse for them. They were very angry at the army for lying, and spent several years trying to find out who decided to tell a lie instead of the truth about Pat's death. Even today, they still have some unanswered questions about the circumstances of his death.

But they knew that even though Pat had died in an accident, he had fought and served honorably. He had not needed to join the army but had chosen to do so because he felt it was the right thing for him to do. It had cost him his life, but Pat Tillman had stayed true to himself. In his honor, Pat's family has since started the Pat Tillman Foundation to aid veterans of the Iraq and Afghanistan wars and their families.

As sportswriter Sarah Kwak later commented in *Sports Illustrated,* "Pat Tillman was a hero. He just wasn't the hero that the U.S. military made him out to be."

## SOURCES AND FURTHER READING

When I write a book, I use many, many different sources, including newspaper stories, magazine articles, books, video documentaries, and the Internet.

If you would like to read more about any of the athletes in this book or the subject of athletes who have served in the military, your teacher or your school or town librarian can probably show you how to find newspaper and magazine articles online. You might also want to look up the books listed below, many of which were helpful to me when writing this book. They may be purchased online or through any bookstore. They might also be in your local library. If not, your library can probably borrow them for you from another library.

Ask your librarian or teacher for help, and remember, the more you read, the easier it becomes.

## TED WILLIAMS

There are many terrific books about Ted Williams. You may want to start with Ted's autobiography, *My Turn at Bat* (Fireside Books, 1988) or Ted's book about batting, *The Science of Hitting* (Fireside Books, 1986). Another good book for younger readers is *Ted Williams: A Portrait in Words and Pictures* by Dick Johnson and Glenn Stout (Walker and Company, 1991). For this book I also used Bill Nowlin's *Ted Williams at War* (Rounder Books, 2007). For more about Ted Williams and the Red Sox, see *The Teammates: A Portrait of Friendship* by David Halberstam (Hyperion, 2003) and *Red Sox Century* by Glenn Stout and Richard A. Johnson (Houghton Mifflin, 2001).

## ROCKY BLEIER

Rocky Bleier's autobiography, *Fighting Back* (Rocky Bleier, Inc., 1998), gives a lot more information on both Rocky's military service and his football career with the Steelers. A movie version of Rocky's story, *Fighting Back: The Rocky Bleier Story,* was made in 1980.

## CARLOS MAY

No one has ever written a book about Carlos May. Two articles from the magazine *Baseball Digest,* "Carlos May Wins the Biggest Game of All" by Jim Murray, October 1970, and "Can Carlos May Make It Back?" by Harold Kaese, December 1969, were useful to me in writing his story, as were newspaper stories from Chicago newspapers. Carlos's story is also told in Rick Swaine's book *Beating the Breaks: Major League Ballplayers Who Overcame Disabilities* (McFarland and Company, 2004).

## PAT TILLMAN

There really isn't a book about Pat Tillman designed for younger readers. I used magazine and newspaper articles about Pat, as well as Mary Tillman's book, *Boots on the Ground by Dusk* (Modern Times, 2008), and *Where Men Win Glory: The Odyssey of Pat Tillman* by Jon Krakauer (Anchor Books, 2010).

You might also be interested in these books about athletes who have served in the military: *Baseball Goes to War* by William Mead (Broadcast Interview, 1991) and *When Baseball Went to War* by Todd Anton and Bill Nowlin (Triumph Books, 2008).

# ABOUT THE AUTHOR

Growing up outside a small town in central Ohio, Glenn Stout never dreamed that he would become a writer. Then reading changed his life. As a kid, Glenn played baseball, basketball, and football, but baseball was always his favorite. Glenn studied poetry and creative writing in college and has had many different jobs, including selling minor league baseball tickets, cleaning offices, grading papers for a college, painting houses, and even working as a construction worker and a librarian. Glenn started writing professionally while he was working at the Boston Public Library and has been a full-time writer since 1993. Glenn wrote forty titles in the Matt Christopher Sports Biography series, and every year he edits The Best American Sports Writing collection. Some of Glenn's other books include *Red Sox Century, Yankees Century, Nine Months at Ground Zero,* and *Young Woman and the Sea: How Trudy Ederle Conquered the English Channel and Inspired the World.* He has written or edited more than seventy books, and started the Good Sports series in 2010.

Glenn is a citizen of both the United States and Canada and lives on Lake Champlain in Vermont with his wife, daughter, three cats, two dogs, and a rabbit. He writes in a messy office in his basement, and when he isn't working, he likes to ski, skate, hike in the woods, kayak on the lake, take photographs, read, and visit schools to talk about reading and writing.

For more information on the Good Sports series, see www.goodsportsbyglennstout.com.

# APPENDIX

# TED WILLIAMS'S CAREER STATISTICS

FULL NAME: Ted Williams

BORN: August 30, 1918 DIED: July 5, 2002

HEIGHT: 6'3" WEIGHT: 205 lbs. BATTED: Left THREW: Right

| YEAR | TEAM | AB | HITS | 2B | 3B | HR | RUNS | RBI | BB | AVG. |
|------|------|-----|------|-----|-----|-----|------|------|------|------|
| 1939 | RED SOX | 565 | 185 | 44 | 11 | 31 | 131 | 145 | 107 | .327 |
| 1940 | RED SOX | 561 | 193 | 43 | 14 | 23 | 134 | 113 | 96 | .344 |
| 1941 | RED SOX | 456 | 185 | 33 | 3 | 37 | 135 | 120 | 147 | .406 |
| 1942 | RED SOX | 522 | 186 | 34 | 5 | 36 | 141 | 137 | 145 | .356 |
| 1946 | RED SOX | 514 | 176 | 37 | 8 | 38 | 142 | 123 | 156 | .342 |
| 1947 | RED SOX | 528 | 181 | 40 | 9 | 32 | 125 | 114 | 162 | .343 |
| 1948 | RED SOX | 509 | 188 | 44 | 3 | 25 | 124 | 127 | 126 | .369 |
| 1949 | RED SOX | 566 | 194 | 39 | 3 | 43 | 150 | 159 | 162 | .343 |
| 1950 | RED SOX | 334 | 106 | 24 | 1 | 28 | 82 | 97 | 82 | .317 |
| 1951 | RED SOX | 531 | 169 | 28 | 4 | 30 | 109 | 126 | 144 | .318 |
| 1952 | RED SOX | 10 | 4 | 0 | 1 | 1 | 2 | 3 | 2 | .400 |
| 1954 | RED SOX | 386 | 133 | 23 | 1 | 29 | 93 | 89 | 136 | .345 |
| 1953 | RED SOX | 91 | 37 | 6 | 0 | 13 | 17 | 34 | 19 | .407 |
| 1955 | RED SOX | 320 | 114 | 21 | 3 | 28 | 77 | 83 | 91 | .356 |
| 1956 | RED SOX | 400 | 138 | 28 | 2 | 24 | 71 | 82 | 102 | .345 |
| 1957 | RED SOX | 420 | 163 | 28 | 1 | 38 | 96 | 87 | 119 | .388 |
| 1958 | RED SOX | 411 | 135 | 23 | 2 | 26 | 81 | 85 | 98 | .328 |
| 1959 | RED SOX | 272 | 69 | 15 | 0 | 10 | 32 | 43 | 52 | .254 |
| 1960 | RED SOX | 310 | 98 | 15 | 0 | 29 | 56 | 72 | 75 | .316 |
| TOTAL | | 2292 | 2654 | 525 | 71 | 521 | 1798 | 1839 | 2021 | .344 |

NOTE: Ted Williams missed 1943, 1944, and 1945 due to military service in World War II. He missed portions of 1952 and 1953 due to military service in Korea.

# ROCKY BLEIER'S CAREER STATISTICS

FULL NAME: Robert Patrick Bleier

BORN: March 5, 1946

HEIGHT: 5'11" WEIGHT: 210 lbs.

RUSHING STATISTICS

| YEAR | TEAM | G | ATT | ATT/G | YDS | AVG | YDS/G | TD |
|------|------|---|-----|-------|-----|-----|-------|-----|
| 1980 | PITTSBURGH STEELERS | 16 | 78 | 4.9 | 340 | 4.4 | 21.2 | 1 |
| 1979 | PITTSBURGH STEELERS | 16 | 92 | 5.8 | 434 | 4.7 | 27.1 | 4 |
| 1978 | PITTSBURGH STEELERS | 16 | 165 | 10.3 | 633 | 3.8 | 39.6 | 5 |
| 1977 | PITTSBURGH STEELERS | 13 | 135 | 10.4 | 465 | 3.4 | 35.8 | 4 |
| 1976 | PITTSBURGH STEELERS | 14 | 220 | 15.7 | 1,036 | 4.7 | 74.0 | 5 |
| 1975 | PITTSBURGH STEELERS | 11 | 140 | 12.7 | 528 | 3.8 | 48.0 | 2 |
| 1974 | PITTSBURGH STEELERS | 12 | 88 | 7.3 | 373 | 4.2 | 31.1 | 2 |
| 1973 | PITTSBURGH STEELERS | 12 | 3 | 0.2 | 0 | 0.0 | 0.0 | 0 |
| 1972 | PITTSBURGH STEELERS | 14 | 1 | 0.1 | 17 | 17.0 | 1.2 | 0 |
| 1971 | PITTSBURGH STEELERS | 6 | – | 0.0 | – | – | – | – |
| 1970 | PITTSBURGH STEELERS | 0 | – | 0.0 | – | – | – | – |
| 1968 | PITTSBURGH STEELERS | 10 | 6 | 0.6 | 39 | 6.5 | 3.9 | 0 |
| TOTAL | | 140 | – | 0.0 | 3,865 | 0.0 | 27.6 | 23 |

# CARLOS MAY'S CAREER STATISTICS

FULL NAME: Carlos May

BORN: May 17, 1948

HEIGHT: 5'11" WEIGHT: 200 lbs. BATS: Left THROWS: Right

| SEASON | TEAM | AB | H | 2B | 3B | HR | R | RBI | BB | AVG |
|--------|------|-----|------|-----|----|----|-----|-----|-----|------|
| 1968 | WHITE SOX | 67 | 12 | 1 | 0 | 0 | 4 | 1 | 3 | .179 |
| 1969 | WHITE SOX | 367 | 103 | 18 | 2 | 18 | 62 | 62 | 58 | .281 |
| 1970 | WHITE SOX | 555 | 158 | 28 | 4 | 12 | 83 | 68 | 79 | .285 |
| 1971 | WHITE SOX | 500 | 147 | 21 | 7 | 7 | 64 | 70 | 62 | .294 |
| 1972 | WHITE SOX | 523 | 161 | 26 | 3 | 12 | 83 | 68 | 79 | .308 |
| 1973 | WHITE SOX | 553 | 148 | 20 | 0 | 20 | 62 | 96 | 53 | .268 |
| 1974 | WHITE SOX | 551 | 137 | 19 | 2 | 8 | 66 | 58 | 46 | .249 |
| 1975 | WHITE SOX | 454 | 123 | 19 | 2 | 8 | 55 | 53 | 67 | .271 |
| 1976 | WHITE SOX AND YANKEES | 351 | 91 | 13 | 2 | 3 | 45 | 43 | 43 | .259 |
| 1977 | YANKEES AND ANGELS | 199 | 47 | 7 | 1 | 2 | 21 | 17 | 22 | .236 |
| TOTAL | | 4120 | 1127 | 172 | 23 | 90 | 545 | 536 | 512 | .274 |

# *PAT TILLMAN'S CAREER STATISTICS*

FULL NAME: Patrick Daniel Tillman

BORN: November 6, 1976 DIED: April 22, 2004

HEIGHT: 5'11" WEIGHT: 204 lbs.

NFL DEFENSIVE STATISTICS POSITION: Safety

| YEAR | TEAM | GAMES | TOTAL TACKLES | SOLO | ASSISTS |
|------|------|-------|---------------|------|---------|
| 1998 | ARI | 16 | 74 | 46 | 28 |
| 1999 | ARI | 16 | 34 | 22 | 12 |
| 2000 | ARI | 16 | 144 | 107 | 37 |
| 2001 | ARI | 12 | 92 | 70 | 22 |
| CAREER TOTALS | | 60 | 344 | 245 | 99 |

# GOOD★SPORTS
## BY GLENN STOUT

# *PLAYING FOR THE LOVE OF THE GAME!*

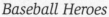

*Baseball Heroes*  *Yes, She Can!*